LILY AND MAIA

A DINOSAUR ADVENTURE

Author Jack Horner

Illustrator Grace Hattrup

Published by Horner Science Group

LILY AND MAIA

NOTES TO PARENTS AND TEACHERS

The state of Montana is filled with many kinds of dinosaurs who lived there eighty million years ago. In this book, I would like to tell you about the very special *Maiasaura*, a kind of duck-billed dinosaur that I discovered many years ago with my friend Bob Makela at Egg Mountain, Montana. We named this dinosaur *Maiasaura*, which means "Good Mother Lizard," when we discovered that she laid eggs in nests and took care of her young babies, bringing them food and protecting them from predatory dinosaurs. Together with James Gorman, I wrote a book about the typical life of a *Maiasaura* called *Maia: A Dinosaur Grows Up*. Now it is time for me to reintroduce you to Maia.

Evidence of dinosaurs' presence on earth for 140 million years comes from their fossilized skeletal remains, footprints, and eggs. By studying these remains and the rocks in which they are found, and then formulating our ideas and theories, paleontologists, such as myself and my colleague Holly Woodward, are able to make educated guesses about what these animals looked like, what they ate, what kind of environments they lived in, and how they behaved and matured.

Lily is an eight-year-old adventurer and amateur paleontologist who loves dinosaurs so much that she can't wait to learn more about how to do field research, and she definitely wants to go to Montana—much like Holly herself when she was a young girl. *Maiasaura* lived and died long before human beings existed—we know this fact, but this is a story about how Lily meets Maia, how they quickly become best friends, and how they travel back in time so that Maia can teach Lily all about how she lived so long ago. Our illustrator, Grace Hattrup (an art student), has done a beautiful job of capturing their adventures.

Both Maia and Lily are the heroines of this story: Maia stands out as a famous dinosaur who has taught scientists much about how dinosaurs lived, and Lily shines because she wants to learn how to do real field research, which may lead to important hypotheses about dinosaurs—even if her discoveries may change some of the ideas Holly and I have published about *Maiasaura* in scientific journals. We see Lily's future as a scientist and paleontologist who searches for the truth about dinosaurs.

And we will continue searching for the truth because that is what scientists do. Never Stop Discovering!

Jack Horner

LILY AND MAIA

CONTENTS

Dedication		4
About Holly Woodward, Ph.D.		5
Lily and Dinosaurs		6
Setting Up Camp		12
Preparation		16
Nighttime Visitors		18
Maia		20
The Adventure Begins		24
Discoveries		30
Time Traveling		34
Worried		38
My Secret Friend		42
Glossary		46
About the Author		47

LILY AND MAIA

THIS BOOK IS DEDICATED TO

HOLLY WOODWARD,

ONE OF MY FORMER DOCTORAL STUDENTS,

AND NOW A UNIVERSITY PROFESSOR WHO STUDIES

MAIASAURA AND HOW DINOSAURS GROW.

LILY AND MAIA

ABOUT HOLLY WOODWARD, Ph.D.

ASSOCIATE PROFESSOR OF ANATOMY AND PALEONTOLOGY
OKLAHOMA STATE UNIVERSITY CENTER FOR HEALTH SCIENCES

Growing up, Holly Woodward was fascinated by all things science and nature, but especially by dinosaurs. By two years of age, she was digging for dinosaur fossils in her front yard with a spoon and pail. Later, when she went off to college at NC State, Holly focused on biology and geology to prepare for a career in paleontology.

It was in graduate school at Texas Tech when she discovered bone histology and was hooked. Microscopic bone structures record the life history of an individual, such as growth rate and age at death. Amazingly, the same stories are preserved in the fossil bones of dinosaurs. Holly wanted to learn even more about bone histology, so she went to Montana State University to study with Dr. Jack Horner.

Jack introduced Holly to *Maiasaura* by showing her fossils that belonged to tiny hatchlings, twenty-foot-long adults, and everything in between. At that time, Jack had already learned lots about *Maiasaura*, especially about the babies. Holly added to Jack's work by studying the histology of fifty individual *Maiasaura* and recording the life story of each individual from the clues in its bone microstructure.

Maiasaura is incredibly special to Holly because it taught her so much about the way a dinosaur lived and grew up–something she had wanted to discover her whole life. As a professor, Holly now teaches her own students about *Maiasaura*, and some of them are working on new research to add even more to the story of this fascinating dinosaur.

CHAPTER 1

LILY AND DINOSAURS

Hi, my name is Lily and I'm a paleontologist. A paleontologist is a person who studies plants and animals that lived a long time ago. I study dinosaurs! Dinosaurs have been extinct for sixty-five million years. Well, that's not exactly true because birds are actually living dinosaurs.

Yep, you heard me right! A hummingbird, a robin, or an ostrich are all cousins of dinosaurs like Tyrannosaurus, Triceratops, or Apatosaurus—and all other kinds of dinosaurs.

LILY AND MAIA

My friend Jack Horner is a paleontologist, too, and he has dug up tons of dinosaurs in Montana. Montana has a lot of them.

One day Jack and his best friend Bob Makela dug up a kind of dinosaur called *Maiasaura*. Actually, Jack and Bob found a whole nesting ground full of these *Maiasaura*. Some nests had eggs in them and some had baby skeletons.

Maiasaura is called a duck-billed dinosaur because they kind of looked like ducks. And they acted like ducks, too, by walking on their hind legs, eating plants, and living in big groups. Sort of like flocks of birds. What an awesome discovery they made!

LILY AND MAIA

I'm about to tell you a story that you won't believe. Are you ready?

Okay, well, after learning about nests of fossilized eggs and baby skeletons, I wanted more than anything to go to Montana to see if I could find a nest of *Maiasaura* myself.

My family knew the people who owned the ranch where Jack and Bob found the *Maiasaura* fossils, and I actually convinced them to take me there as part of our summer vacation!

Our whole family wanted to see the place where *Maiasaura* had lived millions of years ago, and my Mom and Dad liked that I'm so passionate about studying dinosaurs.

CHAPTER 2

SETTING UP CAMP

When we arrived, the ranchers invited us to stay with them in their ranch house. But I wanted to camp outside by myself in the badlands.

If you don't know already, badlands are the dry, rocky areas where fossils are usually found. And exactly where I hoped to find some *Maiasaura* nests.

Mom and Dad were nervous about my idea, but they agreed to my plan because the ranchers said no dangerous animals lived in the area. And I had my cell phone in case of an emergency!

LILY AND MAIA

My mom drove me out to a small stream near the badlands where I could set up my camp, and we made a plan for her to pick me up the next morning.

I was prepared. I took my tent and sleeping bag with me, my fishing pole and some food, and, of course, all my paleontology tools. Plus my cell phone, which I would mostly use to take lots of pictures.

I looked around for a minute—it was a typical Montana summer evening. I could smell sweet grass in the cooling air and saw a beautiful pinkish sky lighting up the hills where the badlands began. I couldn't see any signs of life for miles and miles.

But I wasn't lonely or scared at all.

LILY AND MAIA

I set up my tent and gathered some sticks of wood to build my campfire and then went down to the stream to catch some fish for my dinner. I got lucky in the first five minutes and caught a brook trout! Brook trout are little and the perfect size for my frying pan. After I cleaned the trout, I cooked it and had a nice dinner of fish and vegetables and a brownie my Mom had made for me as a surprise treat.

CHAPTER 3

PREPARATION

After dinner I took the tools out of my backpack to make sure I had everything I would need for my field work in Montana.

To find dinosaurs, you need a lot of things: a geology map to identify the different kinds of rocks; a GPS to know your exact location; a little pick, rock hammer, and chisel for digging; a small whisk broom and paint brush to brush the dirt off; and a notebook and pencil to record your findings. You also need some toilet paper to wrap fossils in and plastic baggies to keep the wrapped-up specimens safe and sound.

And don't forget a black marker to label the baggies so you can remember what's inside.

LILY AND MAIA

After making sure I had everything, I returned all the tools to my backpack and hung it on a tree branch so no critters would get inside.

I was so tired when I finally got in my tent that I don't even remember getting into my sleeping bag and falling into a deep sleep.

CHAPTER 4

NIGHTTIME VISITORS

In the middle of the night, I was woken up by coyotes, far off in the distance, howling at the moon. But I wasn't worried because I knew they were just singing their nighttime songs. Listening more closely, I heard other sounds like wind blowing past the tent off and on, and the sound of crickets.

I could also hear what sounded like a small animal scurrying around where I had built my campfire. I was pretty sure that it was a mouse eating up the crumbs of food I had dropped in the dirt.

LILY AND MAIA

As I listened, I heard another sound, but it was very different than anything I had ever heard before. It was like a chirp, but not a bird, and not a cricket. Was this odd chirp moving closer to my tent?

No mistake, the chirp had footsteps now, which were definitely getting closer. The steps stopped just outside my tent door, and there was a different sound now. A cooing sound. Almost like the cooing of a baby.

CHAPTER 5

MAIA

I quietly got out of my sleeping bag, found my flashlight, and pulled back the tent door. Shining the light toward the campfire, where only a few small flames were still burning, I could just make out the shape of an animal curled up alongside the rocks that lined the fire pit.

The animal opened its two big eyes and looked straight at me, but it didn't move. It just looked for a little while, then closed its eyes and made that cooing sound and seemed to just go to sleep. Was I dreaming? I must be, so I plopped back down and fell back to sleep.

LILY AND MAIA

The next time I opened my eyes it was morning, and as I lay there, I remembered that creature with its big eyes staring at me in the middle of the night. I decided to peek outside.

To my amazement, next to the fire pit was the night creature still sound asleep! It was green with yellow spots, and it looked pretty darn big.

LILY AND MAIA

As I climbed out of the tent, the creature opened its eyes wide and lifted its head. It made its cooing sound again and pushed itself up into a standing position. Wow, I thought, it's bigger than me!

Wait, I suddenly realized exactly what I was looking at—a baby dinosaur! Yes, the creature I saw during the night was actually a baby duck-billed dinosaur. A baby *Maiasaura!*

CHAPTER 6

THE ADVENTURE BEGINS

"What are you doing here?" I said out loud. "Am I dreaming? Dinosaurs are extinct. There's NO WAY we can be here together right now!"

The baby dinosaur just stood there, cooing. My mom always tells me that sugar before bedtime makes people dream. I was pretty sure I was still dreaming because I ate that brownie after dinner.

LILY AND MAIA

I stepped up to the baby *Maiasaura* and asked, "Can I touch you?"

The baby just cooed and stayed very still while keeping her eyes on me.

"Wow, your skin is bumpy but really soft."

LILY AND MAIA

Then, the baby *Maiasaura* started walking away toward the badlands. After a few steps, she stopped and looked back at me. I think she wanted me to follow her. Should I?

It was a pretty easy decision, so I grabbed my backpack and caught up to her, and she turned and started walking again towards the badlands. And I followed.

As we walked side by side, I introduced myself. "My name is Lily. You look like a *Maiasaura*. Can I call you Maia?"

Maia turned toward me and cooed. By now, I was pretty sure the cooing sound meant something good, so I smiled at this cute dinosaur as we walked into the badlands. I thought to myself, this is the best dream I have ever had!

LILY AND MAIA

After we walked about two hundred steps, Maia stopped suddenly and squatted on the ground.

"What is it, why did you sit down, Maia?"

Maia stuck out her left arm and put her duck-like beak on the ground next to her hand. When I looked down at the spot where she was pointing, I saw a whole bunch of broken, black dinosaur eggshells.

"Wow," I cried, "those are dinosaur eggshells! Maia, are those your broken eggs?"

CHAPTER 7

DISCOVERIES

Maia turned her head away from the eggshells and made a soft chirping sound. "Hmm," I asked, "are these your relatives' eggshells?" Maia turned her head back toward me and cooed. I smiled and thought to myself, I can't believe I'm talking with a dinosaur!

I had a lot of questions for her as we sat there next to the eggshells. "Maia, where did you come from? I can't understand how you can be here. Can you show me where you live?"

LILY AND MAIA

Maia cooed and stood up and began walking further into the badlands. And I of course followed her. After about another two hundred steps, we came to a small canyon lined with chokecherry bushes.

Maia cooed and stripped off a bunch of berries and ate them. I reached out to pick some and ate them, too. "Yum, these are really good."

LILY AND MAIA

As I picked a few more berries, Maia crept deeper into the canyon, where the chokecherry bushes were much thicker. I had to run to catch up and stay with her so we wouldn't lose each other. Maia was the same color as the bushes and very hard to see—basically she blended right in.

After fighting our way through all those chokecherry bushes, we popped through to the other side and found ourselves in an open area at the end of the canyon, against a wall of rock with a large crack-like cave.

CHAPTER 8

TIME TRAVELING

Maia walked up to the giant crack and squeezed right into it. Oh my gosh, I thought to myself, where is Maia going now? When Maia's tail disappeared into the crack, I stuck my head inside and could see that it opened up. Maia was just standing there, cooing. Yikes, but I stepped inside!

The cave was dark, but I could see some rays of light further ahead, and Maia started walking toward the light. I thought to myself, Mom and Dad probably wouldn't be too happy about me doing this. But I just have to see where Maia is going. This is much too important for paleontology.

LILY AND MAIA

After fifty more steps, we both saw another crack in the rock. I could hear a lot of noise coming from the other side and felt a warm breeze coming through. It was very bright like the sun was shining.

Maia squeezed through this crack, too, and then turned to watch me as I climbed through the opening. Then she moved quickly out of my way so I could see where she brought me!

LILY AND MAIA

We were on a hillside above a big open field surrounded by very large pine trees. At the bottom of the hill, and only about three hundred steps away from us in that open field, was a group of twenty huge *Maiasaura* parents all tending nests containing little baby dinosaurs. The noise was SO SO loud! There were loud honking sounds and a whole lot of chirping and some cooing.

I just stood there and stared! "Oh my gosh, this is so awesome!" And my friend Maia cooed back at me.

CHAPTER 9

WORRIED

I stood there, too stunned to say much at first. "This is so amazing!" Maia cooed again. Time for some field photos. I reached into my backpack for my phone. What? No signal. The clock was frozen, too. Uh-oh.

I had so much to do. But I started to get worried and wanted to get back to camp.

"Maia, I have to return to the badlands because who knows what time it is, and my Mom and Dad will worry about me."

LILY AND MAIA

I took a few last photos of the nesting ground and gave Maia a big hug around her soft, nubby neck. "I have to go back but I'll come visit again very soon! Thank you so much for showing me where you come from. I know that I'm probably dreaming, but this is the best dream I have ever had in my whole life!"

I crawled back through the crack, ran to the other side of the cave, and climbed out the other side, pushing my way through the chokecherry bushes until I was back in the badlands.

LILY AND MAIA

I went back to where Maia had shown me the eggshells and picked up all the little pieces, carefully wrapping them in toilet paper and putting them into one of the plastic baggies I had in my backpack.

I remembered to label it with the black marker and wrote down the date, the GPS location, and the information that its contents had been discovered by Maia and collected by me.

CHAPTER 10

MY SECRET FRIEND

After carefully returning the baggie to my backpack, I headed back to camp and called my mom.

"Hi, Mom, it's me. I just wanted to let you know I'm doing good. This is the best time I have ever had being a paleontologist! I have to come back here more this summer, and next summer, and the summer after that, and...."

LILY AND MAIA

"Lily, slow down," Mom said. "Dad and I are really happy you're having fun, but by next year you may want to go explore some other place that has dinosaur fossils."

"No, I can promise you that I will always want to come back here to Montana, Mom. In just this one day I think I discovered evidence that Dr. Jack Horner was wrong about how close together *Maiasaura* dinosaurs nested from one another. He said the nests were separated by the length of one adult, but I saw proof that the nests were a lot closer than that."

LILY AND MAIA

"Well Lily," my Mom said, "you will have to take that discussion up with Dr. Horner because neither your father nor I can argue that one with you. You're the paleontologist in our family, and I am sure you know what kind of evidence you need to make a good scientific argument."

"Should we come to get you now?"

"No, Mom, PLEASE let me stay out another day or two. There are so many things to discover here, and the fishing is good and there are some yummy chokecherries, so I can get plenty to eat!"

LILY AND MAIA

GLOSSARY

Coyote: A species of canine, smaller than its close relative, the wolf. It is native to North America and a predatory animal.

Duck-billed dinosaur: A common name given to the hadrosaurs because of their duck-like beaks. There were many varieties of duck-billed dinosaurs, some of which had hollow crests on the tops of their heads. Duck-billed dinosaurs, or hadrosaurs, have been found all over the world and were probably the most common kind of dinosaur. Duckbills ate plants and were probably the only reptiles that chewed their food instead of swallowing it whole.

Embryo: A baby that has not yet been born. This could be a human baby or a dinosaur baby, which would be located inside of an egg.

Extinct: Describes anything that no longer exists.

Fossil: Is anything that is left, like an impression or actual remains of a once-living thing from a past geological age.

Geology map: Also called a geologic map and shows various geological features like rock units or geologic layers, which are shown by colors and symbols. Paleontologists use these maps to help determine where dinosaurs might be found.

GPS location: Your exact location on earth.

Maiasaura: A kind of duck-billed dinosaur, or hadrosaur, found in western Montana. *Maiasaura* means "good mother lizard." Newly hatched maiasaurs were only fourteen inches long and weighed about one and a half pounds. Yearlings, like Maia in this book, were about eight feet long and weighed about two hundred pounds. Full grown, they were about thirty feet in length and weighed around around three tons.

Montana: A state in North America, located between Idaho and North Dakota, with Canada to the north. The Rocky Mountains run through Montana, and there are many important geological locations for discovering information about the past. It is one of the most active places to look for dinosaurs, but there are also many other locations around the world.

Nesting Ground: A place where animals nest in colonies or groups to lay their eggs and care for their babies.

Paleontologist: A scientist who studies the remains of extinct or fossil life. A vertebrate paleontologist studies the skeletons of fossil animals and an invertebrate paleontologist studies animals that do not have any bones at all.

Scientific hypothesis: An idea based on physical evidence. A scientific argument is a scientific hypothesis.

LILY AND MAIA

ABOUT THE AUTHOR

John R. Horner, known to most people as "Jack," is a world-famous paleontologist known for his fieldwork and research on dinosaur growth and behaviors, and his important discoveries of the first dinosaur eggs and embryos in the Western Hemisphere and the first evidence of dinosaurs nesting in colonies and taking care of their babies.

"Never Stop Discovering" describes Jack's attitude, an outlook formed as a young boy growing up in the plains of Montana. School was difficult for Jack because he is dyslexic, so he headed to the hills every chance he got to look for dinosaur bones. In those hills, Jack discovered dinosaurs and he discovered science.

When Jack was in high school, he won the regional science fair for comparing dinosaurs from Montana and Canada. He went on to become a ground-breaking scientist and was granted an honorary doctorate degree from the University of Montana and received many awards in his long career, including a lifetime achievement award from the Society for Vertebrate Paleontology. He has been listed in Newton Graphic Magazine's top twenty-four leading world scientists. And four dinosaurs have been named after him!

Jack worked with Universal Studios to imagine the Jurassic Park and Jurassic World dinosaurs and helped with the premier of the first Jurassic Park film in London with Diana, Princess of Wales, and Steven Spielberg.

Jack has written two books and coauthored seven books on dinosaurs, including three books for children.

Today he teaches at Chapman University, continues his research on dinosaurs, including the "Dino-Chicken" project, and works with Horner Science Group to bring new dinosaur stories and experiences to the world.

In his spare time, he studies the stars and Earth's landscapes and takes a lot of photographs. He also plays with his favorite dinosaur, a parrot named Birdy.

LILY AND MAIA

Copyright © 2023 John R. Horner

All rights reserved. No part of this book may be reproduced or used in any manner without the prior written permission of the copyright owner, except for the use of brief quotations in a book review.

To request permission, contact the publisher at:
Connect@HornerScienceGroup.com

ISBN Number: 979-8-9860630-0-3

First Hardback Cover Edition February 2023

Illustrations by Grace Hattrup
Editing by Marcelle O'Connell
Book Design by Andrea Lynch
Marketing and Promotion by Clare Ochoa

"A special thanks to Audrey O'Connell
for coordinating the publishing of this book." *Jack Horner*

Printed by Ingram Spark

Published by Horner Science Group
4225 Lytle Road N.E., Bainbridge Island, Washington 98119
+1.206.639.9604
https://jackhornersdinosaurs.com
https://www.hornersciencegroup.com

www.ingramcontent.com/pod-product-compliance
Lightning Source LLC
LaVergne TN
LVHW070408070526
838199LV00017B/539